Sunkissed Print
© Copyright 2021 - Joseph and Shaday M. Lackey
All Rights Reserved.
ISBN: 978-1-7356762-5-8
No part of this book may be reproduced or transmitted in any form or by any means; graphic, electronic, or mechanical, including photocopying, recording, taping, or by any information storage retrieval system without written permission of the author.
Printed in the United States of America

Dedication

This book is dedicated to everyone who has the spirit of progress and those who have accepted the responsibility of freedom.

Kwanzaa Celebration

Family Guide

December 26th – January 1st

Created by Joseph Lackey & Shaday M. Lackey

WHAT IS KWANZAA?

Kwanzaa is a cultural holiday that celebrates the past, connects the present, and creates an actionable plan for the future.

The focus of this holiday is on the individual as they relate to the family unit.

Individuals make families. Families make communities. Communities make neighborhoods. Neighborhoods make societies.

The weakness or strength of the individual has a direct impact on the family which causes a ripple that flows throughout.

Kwanzaa Celebration

This celebration begins on December 26th and continues for seven days ending on January 1st.

Much like other holidays, there are season's greetings but also call and response is used.

Season's Greetings:
Heri Za Kwanzaa
(HEAD- DEE- ZAH KWAHN-ZAH)
The phrase means "Happy Kwanzaa" which is like someone saying Merry Christmas.

Call and Response:
Habari Gani
(HAH-BAH-REE GAH-NEE)

- An informal greeting meaning "What's the news?"

- The person would then reply with the Kwanzaa principle for that day.

KWANZAA DECORATIONS

The colors of Kwanzaa are red, black, and green. So let your "Kuumba" guide you in how you make the holiday special to you!

Setting the Kwanzaa Table:
When setting the table, you will need a

- ☐ mkeka (*straw mat*)
- ☐ kinara (*candleholder*)
- ☐ harvest basket
- ☐ kikombe cha umoja (*unity cup*)
- ☐ mazao (*fresh fruits/vegetables*)
- ☐ mushundi (*ears of corn*; one per child)
- ☐ three red candles
- ☐ three green candles
- ☐ one black candle
- ☐ the bendera (red/black/green flag)

Note: The placement and order of the candles teach and reinforce valuable lessons for the family.

Have multiple sets of candles ESPECIALLY the black candle as you will light it more often than the other candles

Kwanzaa Presents

Kwanzaa Gift Giving:
Zawadi or gift-giving is also a part of the celebration.

To paraphrase the words of Fredrick Douglass, it is easier to build strong children than to repair broken adults.

From that basis, the holiday's focus of gift-giving is directed towards children and youth.

The goal of each gift is to help reinforce the current principles and reward them for completion of prior-year Kwanzaa commitments.

Though gifts may vary, items such as a book or anything that encourages learning should also be given. When selecting your gift, consider those items that emphasize education, an understanding of heritage, and reinforces our culture.

KWANZAA DINNER

Karamu (Feast/Banquet) and Celebration:

The Karamu is a special event, the banquet of Kwanzaa. This is when family and friends gather with plenty of food, fellowship, and a time when revisiting the principles and setting goals with family/friends should happen.

Below are elements suggested to be a part of your Karamu:
Welcoming – showing appreciation for attendees especially elders
Reflections – informative or entertaining presentations; discussions about the importance of family and goal recommitments
Thankfulness – showing appreciation for everything that has shaped us, who we are today, and what we will become
Libation Statement – This should happen before the meal and should recognize where we come from, those who came before us, those who come after us, and everything we work towards (sample statement included in the Kuumba libation statement).

Most importantly, Karamu is about celebrating African American culture. It's a time to be thankful for those who are working to make our lives better, those who have passed away, and those who have come before (ancestral roots). By incorporating both African and African American themes, we acknowledge our complete heritage which makes us whole individually and as a people. This banquet celebrates our past, our present, and our future. So have fun, connect, and raise the bendera with pride as you build strong children, strong families, and unite!

Kwanzaa Principles

Kwanzaa Commitments:

Each day represents a principle and character-building block:

Umoja *(unity)* - working together towards the same goal(s).

Kujichagulia *(self-determination)* - self-accountability; leading yourself first and holding yourself accountable.

Ujima *(collective work and responsibility)* - Interdependence; accomplishing more by working with someone towards the same goal(s).

Ujamaa *(cooperative economics)* - making money work for you, your people, and your purposes.

Nia *(purpose)* - finding what "drives" you to make a change and using it to improve our society.

Kuumba *(creativity)* - using your mind to "find a way or make one;" there is no map on the road to change or greatness.

Imani *(faith)* - believing that what you are working towards will happen. Failure isn't final.

Use this as a guide for daily principles and when observing throughout the year. Align individual commitments, based on the principles, into the family's goal(s).

CELEBRATING THE KWANZAA PRINCIPLES

In the next section, we are going to give you an outline to reference how you can frame your Kwanzaa ceremony.

The principles make it cultural your inputs make it special. Make the ceremony special for you and your family.

In my family, we've made presentations honoring deceased relatives, played games, done trivia, and given out prizes for participation. We incorporate the children into the holiday through family talent shows to build confidence and family performances to find another way to bond and work together. Anything is fair game if it's meaningful to your family and serves a greater purpose.

Each day, a ceremony takes place and includes a special reading. This reading serves as an overview of the day and what it means. It includes a reading of the principle, meaning of the candle that will be lighted, and a libation statement in honor of those who have transitioned from this side of life.
Candle abbreviations:

The following abbreviations in the next section mean as follows:
Black – Black Candle
IR – Inner Red Candle
IG – Inner Green Candle
SR – Second Red Candle
SG – Second Green Candle
TR – Third Red Candle
TG – Third Green Candle

Day 1 – Umoja (Unity):
OO-MOH-JAH

Reading:
Today is the first day of Kwanzaa - Umoja! This principle encourages both our immediate and extended families to align individual and group goals to one main objective. In doing so, when we improve our lives, we improve the lives of everyone.

Kwanzaa Candle Lighting: Black Candle
This candle represents Black people. We must build the capacity of the individual to strengthen the unity in our families, neighborhoods, communities, and society. Each person should intentionally plan how to become more capable to meet the needs of their family and community.

Libation & Libation Statement:
We pour this libation in remembrance of those who have gone before us. Their success paved the way, their failures taught us lessons. We recognize all generations of mothers and fathers, grandparents, aunts, uncles, siblings, spouses, and friends. (Pour libation)

Day 2 – Kujichagulia
(Self-Determination/Self-Accountability):
KOO-JEE-CHAH-GOO-LEE-AH

Reading:
Today is the second day of Kwanzaa – K*ujichagulia!* We must learn to hold ourselves accountable for failures, successes, progress, and stagnation. Once we learn to address our problems, our problems will be solved. If we do not learn to use ourselves effectively, someone else will gladly do so.

"If you borrow a man's leg, you'll go where he directs you."
African Proverb

Kwanzaa Candle Lighting: Black and Inner Red Candle
The red candle symbolizes your determination, work, and effort. It reminds us to reflect on what is required of us to realistically reach our goals. Both children and adults should strive to be productive, contributive, and accountable.

Libation & Libation Statement:
We pour this libation in remembrance of those who have gone before us. Their success paved the way, their failures taught us lessons. We recognize all generations of mothers and fathers, grandparents, aunts, uncles, siblings, spouses, and friends. (Pour libation)

Day 3 – Ujima (Collective Work & Responsibility):
OO-JEE-MAH

Reading:
Today is the third day of Kwanzaa – *Ujima*. This principle focuses our efforts on collective work and responsibility or ***interdependence***. Dependence is ***waiting*** for ***someone or something*** to do the work. Independence is doing all the ***work alone.***
Interdependence is ***working together*** with independent people. Interdependence can only be achieved when independent people act together to reach goals and make a positive impact.
Ujima encourages openness to constructive criticism and evaluation from others as it relates to common goals. Despite our differences, collective work and effort drive exponential results which is the most effective way forward.

"Two men in a burning house must not stop to argue."
Ghanian Proverb

Kwanzaa Candle Lighting: Black, Inner Red, Inner Green
This candle represents our future success and achievement.

Libation & Libation Statement:
We pour this libation in remembrance of those who have gone before us. Their success paved the way, their failures taught us lessons. We recognize all generations of mothers and fathers, grandparents, aunts, uncles, siblings, spouses, and friends. (Pour libation)

Day 4 – Ujamaa (cooperative Economics):
OO-JAH-MAH

Reading:

Today is the fourth day of Kwanza – *Ujamaa*. Ujamaa promotes the principle of cooperative economics - making our money work for our people and purposes. "Buying Black" a few times is not enough. We must build institutions that provide value for all communities, use a portion of the profits to build more institutions, and by doing so create systems that serve our purpose to reach our goals. The foundation for that model should originate in the family. Direct your children to work together to produce results, providing the framework for what they should do throughout their lives.

Kwanzaa Candle Lighting: Black, IR, IG, SR

This candle symbolizes our commitment to collective work and effort.

Libation & Libation Statement:

We pour this libation in remembrance of those who have gone before us. Their success paved the way, their failures taught us lessons. We recognize all generations of mothers and fathers, grandparents, aunts, uncles, siblings, spouses, and friends. (Pour libation)

Day 5 - Nia (Purpose):
NEE-YAH

Reading:

Today is the fifth day of Kwanzaa – *Nia*. Nia encourages us to uncover what motivates us to want more in life.

> ***"The ruin of a nation begins in the homes of its people."***
> ***Ghanian Proverb***

Likewise, the development of the nation also begins in the home. Uncovering your drive for more and aligning that to make our society better will directly benefit you and everyone in our society.

Kwanzaa Candle Lighting: Black, IR, IG, SR, SG

This candle symbolizes our motivation to shape the future, build financial strength, and improve our community.

Libation & Libation Statement:

We pour this libation in remembrance of those who have gone before us. Their success paved the way, their failures taught us lessons.
We recognize all generations of mothers and fathers, grandparents, aunts, uncles, siblings, spouses, and friends. (Pour libation)

Day 6 – Kuumba (Creativity):
KOO-OOM-BAH

Reading:

Today is the sixth day of Kwanzaa – Kuumba. This principle encourages us to find creative solutions for our problems. It is up to everyone to be creative in finding or making a way to reach our goals. This principle combined with the others will produce levels of change that no one imagined possible.

"Do not follow the path. Go where there is no path to begin a trail."
Ghanaian Proverb

Kwanzaa Candle Lighting: Black, IR, IG, SR, SG, TR
This candle represents the creativity and ingenuity that we all possess and require to bring lasting change.

Libation & Libation Statement:
We pour this libation in remembrance of those who have gone before us. Their success paved the way, their failures taught us lessons.
We recognize all generations of mothers and fathers, grandparents, aunts, uncles, siblings, spouses, and friends.
The plant symbolizes our efforts in the outside world. For it to bear fruit, we must consistently take offensive action (having the correct soil or environment, watering) and defensive action (pulling weeds or unwanted results). If we pause or stop for too long, everything up to that point can be overrun and lost. Remain steadfast and dedicated to improving the lives of ourselves, our family, community, and society. In honor of all of whom are important to us, we pour this libation.
(Pour libation)

Day 7 – Imani (Faith):

EE-MAH-NEE

Reading:
Today is the final day of Kwanza and the first day of the new year. *Imani,* the "Day of Meditation." Faith is the ultimate sustainer as it keeps us moving from impossible to possible.

Faith can also be viewed as "a positive attitude." Without faith, nothing is possible. With it, nothing is impossible. We must believe in ourselves, one another, and our ability to solve our issues to reach our goals.

No matter how bad it looks, or how long it takes, if we keep the faith WHILE working, WE WILL OVERCOME.

Kwanzaa Candle Lighting: Black, IR, IG, SR, SG, TR, TG
This candle represents faith in our work to make a positive and lasting change.

Libation & Libation Statement:
We pour this libation in remembrance of those who have gone before us. Their success paved the way, their failures taught us lessons. We recognize all generations of mothers and fathers, grandparents, aunts, uncles, siblings, spouses, and friends. (Pour libation)

KWANZAA ACTIVITY SUGGESTIONS

UMOJA (December 26th)

❧   Engage in any activity that centers on or reinforces family togetherness (ex. eating together, movies, park, exercising, etc.).

❧   Write down one goal your family can work together to achieve.

❧   Give yourself Swahili names. It is a fun process and meaningful activity.

KUJICHAGULIA (December 27th)

❧   Recall times of how self-accountability helped you. Share your family story.

❧   Reflect on a time when self-accountability would have changed the results of an event.

❧   Write down one area you will apply this principle today and throughout the year.

UJIMA (December 28th)

❧   Discuss significant (historical/non-historical) events that demonstrated collective work and/or responsibility.

❧   Discuss how an Interdependent group can do more than a dependent or independent group.

❧   Share your interpretation of the proverb "A bundle cannot be fastened with one hand."

❧   Write down one way you will apply this principle today and during the year. Find someone to work on this goal with you.

UJAMAA (December 29ᵗʰ)

🌀   Discuss ways to create revenue and strengthen the family. (Before you make one million dollars, you must make $100 first.)

🌀   Write down one achievable thing you will do to practice this principle today and throughout the upcoming year.

NIA (December 30ᵗʰ)

🌀   Imagine yourself on your deathbed. What do you regret? What are you proud of? Write down both lists. (This list gives you an idea of what is important to you and what drives you.) Make goals that move towards the best outcome for both you and society.

KUUMBA (December 31ˢᵗ)

🌀   Discuss actionable ways to solve a problem where the answer is not readily available. Test your solutions by implementing them.

🌀   Engage in some creative activities such as crafting, singing, dancing, playing musical instruments, or building something. Make something together!

🌀   The Karamu Feast & Banquet takes place today! Enjoy yourself and the delicious food. This is a time for celebrating the joy of living, love among family and friends, and the achievement of which have been attained during the year.

🌀   Write down one thing you will do to practice this principle today and throughout the upcoming year.

IMANI (January 1ˢᵗ)

🌀   Reflect and meditate on the year ahead.

🌀   Review your Kwanzaa commitments for each principle and record them in a Kwanzaa journal.

🌀   Plan, for yourself and your family, to review your commitments often throughout the year.

INSPIRATIONAL QUOTES

A people without the knowledge of their past history, origin, and culture is like a tree without roots. – *Marcus Garvey*

No matter what accomplishments you make, somebody helped you. – *Althea Gibson*

It is clear that we must find an African solution to our problems, and that this can only be found in African unity. Divided we are weak; united Africa could become one of the greatest forces for good in the world. - *Dr. Kwame Nkrumah*

The only way to get the monkey off your back is to stand straight up – *Dr. John Henrik Clarke.*

If you want to go fast, go alone. If you want to go far, go together. – *African Proverb*

The most common way that people give up their power is by thinking they don't have any. – *Alice Walker*

Money won't create success, the freedom to make it will. – *Nelson Mandela*

The best way to fight an alien and oppressive culture is to embrace your own. - *African Proverb*

The child that's not embraced by the village will burn it down to feel its warmth. – *African Proverb*

Any society that does not succeed in tapping into the energy and creativity of its youth will be left behind. – *Kofi Annan*

We have to talk about liberating minds as well as liberating society. – *Angela Davis*

If you wish to move mountains tomorrow, you must start by lifting stones today. – *African Proverb*

Good Reads

Until the passing of the Civil Rights Act of 1964, racism was legal and accepted widely. This means, anyone born before 1964 was technically raised in and learned the same lessons that upheld slavery in the United States.

We have a lot of ground to cover to get our generations to have love and respect for themselves and others on the mass scale. Below are just a few books to increase the awareness of past situations that impact Black people. Those who can't remember the past will re-live it in the future.

The Mis-Education of the Negro – *Carter G. Woodson*

Brainwashed – *Tom Burrell*

Black Fortunes – *Shomari Wills*

Destruction of Black Civilization – *Chancellor Williams*

The Color of Law – *Richard Rothstein*

The Color of Money – *Mehrsa Baradaran*

Family Kwanzaa Journal Sheet

Kwanzaa

Umoja:

20_____

Kujichagulia:

Ujima:

Ujamaa:

Nia:

Kuumba:

Imani:

~ REPRODUCIBLE ~

Glossary

B

Bendera (BEHN-DEH-RAH) – flag

H

Habari Gani (HA-BAH-REE GAH-NEE) – "What's the news?"

Harambe (HAH-RAHM-BEH) – "Let's pull together!"

I

Imani (EE-MAH-NEE) – faith; day #7

K

Karamu (KAH-RAH-MOO) – feast

Kikombe cha umoja (KEE-KOM-EH-CHAH OO-MOH-JAH) – unity cup

Kinara (KEE-NAH-RAH) – candle holder

Kiswahili (KEE-SWAH-HEE-LEE) – proper name for the Swahili language

Kujichagulia (KOO-JEE-CHAH-GOO-LEE-AH) – self-determination; day #2

Kuumba (KOO-OOM-BAH) – creativity; day #6

Kwanzaa (KWAHN-ZAH) – first fruits

M

Mazao (MAH-ZAH-OH) – fruits and vegetables

Mishumaa saba (MEE-SHOO-MAH SAH-BAH) – seven candles of the kinara

Mkeka (MM-KEH-KAH) – straw place mat

Muhindi (MOO-HIN-DEE) – ears of corn

N

Nuguzo Saba (NN-GOO-ZOH SAH-BAH) - the seven principles

Nia (NEE-AH) – purpose; day #5

S

Swahili (SWAH-HEE-LEE) – a language of East Africa

U

Ujamaa (OO-JAH-MAH) – cooperative economics; day #4

Ujima (OO-JEE-MAH) – collective work and responsibility; day #3

Umoja (OO-MOE-JAH) – unity; day #1

Z

Zawadi (ZAH-WAH-DEE) - gifts

From our family to yours.... Happy Kwanzaa!

We hope this guide has helped you make this celebration special for you and your family!

— The Lackeys (Kiongonzis)

www.ingramcontent.com/pod-product-compliance
Lightning Source LLC
Chambersburg PA
CBHW061123170426
43209CB00013B/1658